Zero to Freedom Secrets

Zero to Freedom Secrets

Break Free & Grow Your Consulting Freedom Business to Over $100k a Year/Month

Bruno Morris

Published by Game Changer Publishing

ISBN: 979-8-9870839-5-6

FREE GIFTS

DOWNLOAD YOUR FREE GIFTS

Read This First

Just to say thanks for buying and reading my book, I would like to give you a few free bonus gifts, no strings attached!

To Download Now, Visit:
www.ZerotoFreedomSecrets.com/Freegifts

ADVANCE PRAISES

"The student becomes a master. Bruno was a student of mine and very quickly went on to grow his business and become a fantastic coach, helping many start and grow their own business. Bruno's passion and relentless desire to help others is a superpower." - **Luca Senatore, co-founder at Genie Goals, founder of Sam Mentoring, Amazon best-selling author of *The Agency***

"I've been working with Bruno for the past two years, and there are a couple of things about him that got my attention when I started working with him: 1- Bruno is a critical thinker; he's one of those people who thinks outside the box. 2- He's a fantastic holistic growth coach. He not only knows about Google Ads, but also Facebook Ads, email marketing, copywriting, funnels, creating an offer, and buyer psychology." - **Antonio Calero, Head of Marketing Services for Hootsuite and AdEspresso**

"I give a ton of credit to Bruno Morris and the work I did with him. I'm excited to see he's realizing his own book. Bruno really opened my eyes to how to build my business, how to scale my business, and what sort of efforts I can do to expand beyond having just one channel to promote my business. I've already got so much value, and he's just a really nice guy, easy to work with, highly available, and has a great team and program." - **Keith Allen Johns, TedX Speaker and Founder of the Solopreneur Launchpad**

"We're just excited to be part of this program with Bruno. We've been it for about a month now, and we can already see the difference in our business and our life! We've already invested in so many programs before working with Bruno, but this one blows the rest out the water" - **Odette And Mark Clayton, Love, Sex & Relationship coaches**

"So I've been working with Bruno for a month, and it looked cool before joining; it was even cooler after I joined. The coolest thing is that in the first two weeks, I made the investment back while launching masterclasses and making them fun!" - **Jade Lotus, Vitality coach and Founder of The Art of The Bed Chamber**

"Massive shoutout to Bruno and his team. I've been in for three weeks now, and not only is it easy to understand (I have three kids, and my brain is fried!), I got 12 clients in the first week following Bruno's consultation, and now I'm fully booked, and I have to turn people away until I employ someone else to help me." - **Chantelle Voller, Managing Director at Chantelle Keller Williams Realty**

DEDICATION

To Rebecca Ossai Faith, my mother, who always prays for me.

*Your prayers and unconditional love always give me the strength
to overcome any obstacles in my way.*

As you always remind me: "The Lord is our shepherd."

To Gloria Merendino, my loving fiancé.

*Your love and care are out of this world. I wouldn't be the man I am without
you. Thank you for always being there, for the support and the belief you have
in me. I am so blessed to share my life with you.*

Zero to Freedom Secrets

Break Free & Grow Your Consulting Freedom
Business to Over $100k a Year/Month

Bruno Morris

GC | Game Changer
PUBLISHING

www.PublishABestSellingBook.com

Table of Contents

Who this book is for, and where to begin?

This book is for you if:

- You have the heart to make the world a better place.
- You feel called to make a difference, but you don't know where to start.
- You currently have a business or want to start one and be free.

Consultants, agency owners, speakers, entrepreneurs, healers, creators, business owners, influencers, teachers, visionaries, and leaders—this book is for you. This book can help you go from wherever you are to making $100k a year/month.

But this book will not be actionable unless you have made a few key decisions. Before beginning, you must first decide *what's your freedom number* (the monthly income you want to achieve to feel free). Decide that you don't want to stay in the same situation you are in right now, but you want to achieve your definition of freedom. And now that you know you don't want to stay in your current situation, but you want to achieve your freedom number, decide you will follow the roadmap to achieve your freedom number and your definition.

This playbook is your roadmap with specific steps to achieve your definition of freedom. Depending on where you are, you could skip some steps of the playbook as each chapter is designed to take you to the next level.

So if you're starting out, you don't have a business, and you don't know where to begin, start from the beginning, and this book will literally take you from zero to your freedom number.

If you already have a coaching/consulting business making more than *$10k* per month, you can skip step 2 and go to step 3.

If your coaching/consulting business is making more than *$20k* per month, you can skip steps 2 & 3 and go to step 4.

If your coaching/consulting business is making more than *$30k* per month, you can skip steps 2, 3 & 4 and go to step 5.

But wherever your business is currently, you don't want to skip steps 1, 5, and 6—you'll understand why☺

Introduction

Almost five years ago, I embarked on a journey to discover the ultimate truth. I've been trying to understand how to overcome that fear of writing that book, launching that personal brand, speaking in public, launching your online business, quitting your nine-to-five to follow your dream and live a life of freedom. In short, three things needed to be done:

Becoming the person you need to be, to **Do** the things you need to do to **Have** the life you really want.

Sometimes I forget how it was at the beginning.

It was April 2018. I was smoking with my friend, and we were so high.

And in that moment is when it exploded, it was like a light bulb literally exploding inside my head. My friend and I were talking about how we recently moved out from Italy to study and master digital marketing in London to find better job opportunities. Italy is beautiful to me. It is probably the best country in the world (I'm Italian-born and raised).

The food is amazing, the weather is amazing, women are amazing (I'm so lucky to be spending my life with my Sicilian fiancé). But there were few job opportunities in Italy, especially if you were working in digital marketing.

So my friend and I discussed the main reasons people feel inadequate when their skills and intelligence are undervalued. We talked about how people can feel unsatisfied when forced to accept a rule that doesn't allow them freedom and that's far away from what they would really love to do. And how people rely a lot on a system that has already let them down. Can you relate to that?

Have you ever felt unhappy and unsatisfied when you're doing a job that doesn't spark your passion, and you know that is not what you're meant to do? Or felt that you couldn't have control over your life, over your time, over where you live? You know that you're here for better things.

You know that you have a bigger mission in this world, and you know that you want to help people to achieve that mission, but you can't because you're stuck in this rat race, working from nine-to-five (or even more than 40 hours a week), trying to pay an increasing avalanche of bills.

I felt like that too. I worked in different digital marketing agencies in London, and I was moving from one agency to another, looking for more.

Then I realized that the problem wasn't the agencies themselves. Some were considered the top marketing agencies in London.

The problem was that my personality wasn't compatible with working in the office. I'm an introvert. I need to recharge after a couple of hours in groups. Imagine doing eight hours in groups. I can't do small talk. I don't do well in group meetings. I get bored working from the same place every day. And I work better alone than in teams. All those "skills" were important to have in my digital marketing roles in the office.

I was a depressed nine-to-fiver trying to make money online. I really wanted to break free and launch my own business so I wouldn't have to to feel trapped in my nine-to-five job

Without even considering my love for traveling and adventures, I believe this unsatisfied situation is one of the reasons that pushed me to start smoking weed.

And this is not an excuse.

I don't recommend smoking weed, even if it is considered by some a gift from God that is natural and should be legalized. I still don't recommend it because, for me, weed was just a way to escape my daily reality, that reality where I felt trapped, I felt unhappy, I felt I couldn't be myself. So smoking weed was my way to escape that reality until that day we were so high, and we had a massive realization.

It literally exploded into the heavens! I saw these beautiful patterns of dancing colors. The air was liquid and fresh, even if it was a hot summer evening in Brighton. And I had that sense of one giant consciousness— *we're all in the same boat. We're all one race, we're all connected, and we all want freedom.*

I wanted to be able to travel, be free and live life on my own terms.

And I wasn't alone.

A lot of my friends wanted that exact freedom.

And I didn't choose to work 40 hours a day, have only 21 days of holiday, and have to live far away from my fiancé. Why couldn't I just choose how I wanted to live?

I just wanted to be in control of my life. Isn't that normal? To work on what you want, when you want, where you want, and for the reasons you want, for your "why."

I wasn't crazy, stupid, or high just because I wanted the freedom to live the way I wanted. And I'm so glad I found so many people who saw it the same way because I realized my mission.

Now, the fact that you're reading this book means a lot to me, and I don't take that lightly.

After that realization five years ago, I decided to start my own journey to go from *zero to freedom*. I wrote this book to make sure that YOU have the exact tools YOU need to go from *zero to freedom*.

This is the book I wish I had 5 years ago. I was making only a few dollars a day online, and many days I actually lost money.

That meant I wasn't able to travel and be free, let alone live life on my own terms.

So if you're stuck in your nine-to-five job, if you're currently doing a job that you don't love, or if you're ambitious and you know that you should and could do better and that you have a passion that you want to share with the world, this is your shortcut.

Your shortcut to go from zero to financial, location, and time freedom, while positively impacting other people in the process.

I'm sharing my story because this might help you see that if I could break free from a nine-to-five and live my life to the fullest, you can too.

I'm an Afro-Italian Londoner with nothing special about me. I came from a humble Nigerian family. And when I say "humble," I mean that sometimes we struggled to reach the end of the month, having a big family of five in a small apartment in a very small city next to Parma.

I can't complain because my mom did her best. Both my parents did their best. My mom was doing two jobs in two different hospitals to make sure we could achieve and make the end of the month, and I'm super grateful. My mother was my biggest inspiration and my biggest help in all the success I have achieved so far.

And now, I want to give back.

That's why after that realization I had five years ago and the massive journey that I have taken so far, I wanted YOU to achieve the same results in the shortest amount of time.

It took me five years, but you can achieve your definition of freedom in five months!

It took me five years because I didn't know how to get rid of those "golden handcuffs," which were holding me back with the "secure" salary at the end of this month, in exchange of my dreams.

And when I finally managed to quit my 9 to 5 the first time, I ended up replacing it with another prison, but this time I had more "bosses" to be accountable to, and less stability.

To make things worse, I felt terrible because everyone thought I was crazy for wanting to live the digital nomad lifestyle. I felt even worse about the situation because I wouldn't be able to give my girlfriend the life I promised her and knew in my heart she deserved. I felt like a failure.

The problem was that my parents didn't approve of my decision to quit my nine-to-five and live life on my own terms. Nor my friends or my managers.

Which meant not having the support of those closest to me, and I started to believe that maybe they were right...

Maybe I was crazy, maybe my dream was just IMPOSSIBLE.

Then, as if by chance, something amazing happened...

Yannick, my cousin, was in Medellin, one of the top digital nomad cities in South America, and he decided to buy me a flight to go and visit him in Colombia.

As soon as I arrived in this tropical chic hostel called " Casa Kiwi," Yannick was chatting to a group of digital nomads who were sharing all the secrets about launching a freedom consulting business!

Most of them seemed intuitive, others were really counterintuitive...

Some had small details that made a huge difference...

Some were completely unexpected...

Since then, I made it a mission to collect all the top secrets from the top entrepreneurs and put them together in a simple roadmap that anyone can follow to achieve their definition of freedom.

I didn't have a step-by-step book like this to help me in those 5 years.

In those five years, I "ten-Xed" my income and "ten-Xed" again and again, from making an average of $2,000 to $20,000 per month, then $100k per month, and now we're approaching our second million-dollar.

I've "ten-Xed" my freedom from having only 20 days of freedom per year. The typical 20 vacation days or "free" days most nine-to-five jobs will give you.

Now, I literally have six months of freedom a year.

I tend to have one week off every month, sometimes 2 weeks off a month.

And the truth is that even while I'm working, it doesn't feel like working because I do what I love when I want, from where I want.

After achieving that income freedom, financial freedom, and location freedom, I now focus on *impact* because that is when you feel truly free, when your job also gives you the fulfillment to help other people. So I've been focusing on helping other "nine-to-fivers" quit their job and live the life that they want by achieving time freedom, location freedom, and financial freedom.

In this book, I'm going to show you step-by-step exactly how I did it and how you can do it too.

STEP 1

Decide

"It always seems impossible until it's done."
-Nelson Mandela

Start With Your "Why"

In your journey from *zero to freedom*, the very first thing that you want to understand is what is your "why." I mean in the deepest and most conscious way possible. Because it's interesting how when you ask people what they *don't* want, they start rattling off a big list of all the things they don't want in their life.

Conversely, when you ask them what they *do* want, there is often a moment of silence, especially if you ask them why they want that. And if you spend the next 20 minutes following this exercise, I promise you will be more successful than 99% of the people out there because 99% of people don't stop and think exactly why they want what they want.

So start with that. Start with "why." Because why is going to be the biggest motivation that helps you to wake up, get out of bed, implement your powerful money routine, and do what you love to impact people.

And this is because we're spiritual beings in human bodies. We follow our spiritual alignment, and we do the things that are aligned with what is our inner motivation. And to find your inner motivation, we're going to do this exercise called *The Seven Levels of Why*, which is simple in reality.

First of all, think specifically about what you want in life. Do you want more income? Do you want more freedom? Do you want more impact?

I'm going to challenge you to think of a way where you can achieve the three of these because, based on the journey that I've done and the hundreds of clients I've worked with, everyone starts with wanting more money.

But in reality, money is just a tool. Why do you want more money? What is the real reason why you want more money? Generally, it's because you want some type of freedom.

There is that freedom of not having a boss who tells you what to do. There is that freedom to wake up wherever and whenever you want. There is the freedom to live wherever you want, like on a beach by the Caribbean Sea with palm views. Or maybe you're a mountain person who wants to live in the wilderness. Maybe you're in love, and your partner is in another country, and you wish you could spend more time with them.

Perhaps you just want to live close to your family. You want to spend more time at home with kids. There are so many definitions of freedom that you might want to achieve. So start by understanding exactly why you want that income.

When you ask yourself why you want that income, you'll start seeing your first level of "why."

What's your freedom number?

Let's do this step-by-step.

First, what is your income objective? And really take some time to think about it.

A lot of the time, when I ask people what their income objective is, they quickly say a number that they think is the right number, something like $10,000 or $100,000 per month.

But why do you want to make $10,000 or $100,000 per month? There is a better way to calculate your exact freedom number, which is to use our Income Freedom Calculator. This will help you to achieve your Freedom Number.

So, what number do you need to make at the end of each month to feel free?

The best way to calculate your freedom number is by using our Income Freedom Calculator, which is an Excel spreadsheet you can download for free at www.ZerotoFreedomSecrets.com/Freegifts.

If you're old school and just need pen and paper, that is fine too. Write down how much the rent or mortgage would be for your dream house.

How much are you paying for your dream car for insurance, monthly payment, fuel, etc.?

Your lifestyle, write down how much you spend on shopping, eating out, going to the movies with your partner or with the family, visiting your parents, whatever. Take the time to write down exactly how much you're spending on each of those things.

If you spend the next 20 minutes, you'll come out with a specific income—that is your freedom number.

That is the number that you need to make per month.

And if you want to be really motivated to achieve that number, think about why you want to achieve that number.

The seven levels of why

Why do you want to achieve that Freedom Number? You're going to come up with something superficial at the beginning, and when you come up with that answer, ask again, why do you want to achieve that? Do this seven times. This is called *The Seven Levels of Why*.

I learned this from one of my first mentors. He first asked me, "Why do you want to make $10k per month?"

My first answer was, "Because I want to quit my nine-to-five job."

Then he asked me, "Why do you want to quit your nine-to-five?"

I said, "Because I want to be free, and I don't want to have a boss telling me what to do."

Then he asked me, "But why don't you want to have a boss tell you what to do?"

I answered, "Because I can focus on what I really want to do."

Then he asked me, "Why do you want to focus on what you really want to do?"

And what happened after that third question, that third level of "why," is instead of giving the answers from my head, I started to give the answers from my heart. So I realized that it was bigger than me. I started to see the connection between me, my fiancée, who I wanted to start a family with, the family values that my mother instilled in me growing up, and the sacrifice that she had made to make sure that we wouldn't have the same difficult life that she had in Nigeria.

So I started to find the answer deep in my soul, and I started to think about my future family. I responded, "I want to focus on what I really want to do so I can have an increased income to sustain my future wife and kids.

He asked, "Why do you want to be able to sustain your future wife and kids?"

I started to go deeper. And I started to see how my mother raised me in an environment that allowed me to get a good education with a master's degree because she invested. She made that huge investment to make sure that I could have my master's degree. This helped me create a business where I could hire a lot of people from Nigeria, making a huge impact on coaches from the United Kingdom, the U.S., and all over the world, which helped them make a bigger impact on their clients.

I realized that after the income and freedom objectives, it becomes more about the impact on myself, my future wife, my future kids, and all the people I could connect with. That is also why I'm writing this book. So this was just my example of determining my level of "why."

I recommend taking the next 60 minutes to discover your seven levels of why because when you do that, you will become unstoppable.

Step number one to go from zero to freedom *is* to just decide.

Many years ago, reading a book by Tim Ferriss, I learned that the word "decision" comes from the Latin word "incisio."

Incision, of course, means "to cut." The prefix "in" means "to cut into." "Decision," with the prefix "de," means "to cut off."

A decision means "to cut off" all other possibilities, which is why most people are afraid of making decisions.

The nature of a decision is that when you decide to do one thing, you are simultaneously choosing not to do an infinite number of other things.

This feeling of loss inherent in a decision will be front and center in your journey from zero to freedom, so here I've listed the three most important decisions to make in order to start:

1.Decide what's your freedom number.

2.Decide what's your big "why" (it should be a "why" that makes you cry).

3.Decide that you will become the person you need to be to do the thing you need to do to achieve your freedom number.

The easiest process to achieve what you want to have is becoming the person you need to be to do the things you need to do to have the things you want to have.

In the next chapter, we will talk about how to become that person. But first, let's reply to a question you might ask yourself, *"Do I want to do this right now?"*

Why now? And why a consulting business?

It is September 26, 2022, as I'm writing this book in my "office" in the Dominican Republic, just in front of the beach with beautiful turquoise water and infinite palm forest… and we're in a period where the consulting business is booming.

Consulting business means that you're consulting someone to achieve the results that they want to achieve. And the interesting thing is that people need that. You may think you need some type of qualification or certification to do that, but you don't.

One of my clients, Jade Lotus, is a vitality & sex coach, although she doesn't have a specific qualification to practice. She has a story of extensive study with very interesting experts from around the world, which qualifies her to help other people feel alive and have a good sex life.

When she started working with us, she was a marketing beginner, and she went from making $1,500 per month to $20,000 per month without a certification.

Another client, Keith Allen Johns, who's a fantastic mentor & TedX speaker, helps other CEOs break free from their nine-to-five. He doesn't have a certification per se, but he has good experience, is very creative, and is very good at what it does. And that is ten times more important than a certification. He officially became a "freedom hacker" after joining my program. He went from $20k to $50k a month in less than three months.

Or another client like Sahil Sehgal, who went from literally making $2,000 per month as an electrician to making $100,000 per month helping people to grow their business with organic marketing (very similar to our business model).

He didn't have any certifications to help others, but he studied with other coaches who were where he wanted to be to learn how to teach the other students who were two steps behind him.

Because in reality, that's the only thing that you need.

None of the clients I mentioned have a certification. They were only two or three steps ahead of their students who wanted to achieve results. It's like climbing a mountain. You don't need to be at the top of the mountain to help someone else get to the summit. You just need to be two or three steps ahead, meaning you're the roadmap—you know the way.

You can show people behind you the road and how to achieve where they want to be. You can offer your hand and help them to go higher.

That is what you're doing as a consultant. And after Covid, after 2022, this business has been booming, and it will keep growing. There are many projections that the consulting market will reach $1,320.9 billion by 2026.

The best time to start was yesterday. The second best time is now.

And it all starts with the *Optimal You*.

STEP 2

The Optimal You

"In order to build a better business, I had to build a better me"
-Sabri Suby

Build a better you

So let's get this straight. There is someone who already has the dream life that you want to have, already has the dream house that you want to have, already has the dream sex that you want to have, already has the dream relationship that you want to have, already has the financial freedom that you want to have, and already has the location freedom that you want to have. The reality is that someone is exactly like you. He or she has a brain exactly like you; the cell composition is exactly like yours. The only difference is that he or she already became the person they need to be to do the things they need to do to have the dream they want. It all starts by becoming that person.

That's why in this chapter, we're going to talk about how to become the *optimal you*, and that includes three things. As you've noticed, I always talk about the three things for each step because, first, three is the perfect number. Probably because of the Trinity, but I don't want to get into a religious discussion. Three is also the perfect number to remember—it's not too little, and it's not too many. It's perfect.

So, after you have your "why'" and your freedom number objective, to create the optimal you, you need to focus on three things: your non-negotiable, your victory hour, and your bed routine. Let me break those down by first telling you a story.

At the beginning of 2022, I was broke. I was living in this fantastic house in the Dominican Republic, but something went sideways. I had some issues in my relationship, which also impacted my business.

I lost my "why."

I wasn't focused on my objective.

I wasn't aligned with my mission.

I wasn't the *optimal me* anymore, and that made a massive difference in my business, in my body, in my heart, and in my soul. So at the beginning of 2022, I decided to take this back. And it's funny how I went from being broke at the beginning of the year to winning my first million-dollar award called The Two Comma-Club, because I made $1 million by helping other people grow their income, impact, and grow their freedom.

I want to show you exactly how I achieved that and how you can achieve the same.

Your three non-negotiables

The journey to become the "optimal you" starts with setting your non-negotiable because, during this journey, there are going to be distractions, temptations and shiny objects that might hold you back from becoming that person, from doing the things that you need to do, from having the things that you want.

It's important that before you start the journey, you set your non-negotiable.

My number one non-negotiable is prayer.

I'm very religious. In fact, my second name is Chinedu, which means "the Lord is my shepherd." So I believe that everything I have, everything I am, and everything I do is thanks to God. The first thing I do when I open my eyes is give thanks to God for being here and alive. This is the first thing I do every morning because it helps me to ground and be aligned with who I am and what I want to do.

My second non-negotiable is freedom. I started this journey because I wanted to be free from the nine-to-five rat race, free from the boss, free from dogmas, and free from what society tells me I *need* to do. So I always make sure that I'm aligned with that every single morning.

And funny enough, in order to have freedom, it's important to have a bit of structure.

One of the structures I recommend is deep work, a three-hour focus session entering "the zone" where there are no other distractions.

We'll talk more about this in the next step when we talk about productivity power.

And the third non-negotiable for me is love. It can be just as little as a caress or a kiss on my fiancée's cheek, calling my mom to pray together and to wish her well, or calling my brothers to check how they are, or texting a friend, or showing appreciation to my team…

To be honest, it can also be hugging a tree… just some sort of love every day.

I make sure that all those three things happen every day.

Now it is your turn, what are your three non-negotiables?

The Victory Hour

The second essential element that helped me go from zero to a million $ in less than 23 months was having a powerful morning routine.

The first hour in the morning is absolutely the most important, and is called the "victory hour."

I want you to understand that when you give something a powerful name, you're more motivated to do it.

Split your Victory Hour (ideally 5 a.m. to 6 a.m.) into three 20-minute slots, first through movement (intense exercise), then through a period of reflection and solitude, and then through a period of personal growth and/or education.

So, my victory hour consists of three things (again, three is always the perfect number): 20 minutes of meditation, 20 minutes of running and 20 minutes of what I call "killing that little bitch" in your head.

Let's break it down. This is called "victory hour" because when you finish this first thing in the morning, you will feel invincible.

I know that some people have very long morning routines, but in reality, in the morning you have the most precious hours, so it is better to make the most of them.

That's why when I first wake up, I focus on 20 minutes of meditation because this helps me to align with my purpose, feel grateful and it helps me to remember who I am and what I do in this world.

Second, I do 20 minutes of moving because when you wake up, your body is still "sleeping," so a 20-minute run can wake it up. You can run around your neighborhood, along the beach (my favorite), in a park, wherever. You can even just walk up and down the stairs in your house/condo.

Don't use the lack of a gym as an excuse.

Water is my element, so I do it right by the beach.

I like to finish these 20 minutes of moving by entering into the cold water. A cold shower also works if you don't live by the beach. :)

And the final task of my victory hour is the most important one, "killing that little bitch voice" in your head. Because we all have that little voice that tries to hold us back.

That is our ego, **that is the lower self, the opposite of our higher self.**

A lot of times, it's scared. So it starts to hold you back; it needs external approval. It tells you that you are not able to do the things that you need to do to have the things you want.

There is a very easy and powerful exercise to help you kill that voice—it's literally having a conversation with your voice. This conversation can happen in writing. If you're someone like me that loves writing through journaling, where you write down what is the thing that you're grateful for first, what are the things you achieved, and what are the goals you want to achieve? If there is a little voice trying to stop you from achieving those, you need to cage that voice.

You need to tell that voice that you can do it, that you are worth it, that you are strong enough.

You can do this using powerful affirmation as well.

When you cage that little voice in your head is when you're free.

Implementing this "victory hour" in your routine will help you get closer and closer to that optimal you, to that person that you need to be to do the things you need to do to have the things you want.

And finally, during this process, I watch my "mind movie" while drinking my protein shake or hot beverage.

This "mind movie" is one of the most powerful mind hacks you can have to hack your brain and become the person you need to be. A "mind movie" is a video created by you where you are the protagonist (this video can be easily done with any video application).

You can edit a picture of yourself already achieving the things you want: a picture of yourself already living in your dream house, already having the perfect relationship you want to have, and already delivering the impact you want to deliver.

It's a movie of yourself in the future where you are the star, and you already have the things you want.

If you watch that "mind movie" every morning, it hacks your brain and convinces you that you already became that person as the brain can't tell the difference between what is real and what is imaginary.

You're convincing your brain that you are already the person you need to be.

Bed routine

Finally, you want to have **a powerful bed routine** because you're going to have a very impactful period if you follow this playbook. If you're still in your nine-to-five, you might need to do some extra work during this period.

So to start your journey to achieve your freedom, it's important to have a very powerful routine. Make sure that you never feel bored, you never feel stressed, and you're always alive.

The last part of the daily routine, I call the "three, two, one." Because at the end of the day, you might still be thinking about your business, or maybe you work right up to the time your head hits the pillow, and while you're lying in bed, your eyes are open, and your head is just spinning, right? The wheels are still turning, and you're just thinking about your business. Ultimately, it's going to lead to burnout. Not after one month, one week, or two weeks. It's probably more like one to two months that you're going to start burning out if you treat your business and your life like this. And that's why having this end-of-day routine is important. If you don't have a natural stop, you're always thinking about your work, the online business you're creating, and everything you want to do. And there's not going to be any division between your personal life and your professional life. Everything gets jumbled into one.

More importantly, performance is not going to be good. You're not going to experience the freedom you want because you're not going to recover properly at night time.

This exercise to end your day is very simple. It takes you about 90 seconds to do it. You can try it now, then make sure you implement it and do it every evening, so it becomes a habit.

Speaking of habits, a little later, I'm also going to show you how to implement a habit tracker to make sure that these things become a habit and that you will implement them easily into your life.

Again, this is called the "three, two, one," and you're going to write down three things that you're grateful for that happened during the day, okay? This is also connected to the morning thing because a lot of the time, when you start your day, after you've done your non-negotiable, the first thing you can do is read the *three* things that you are grateful for from the day prior, in case you can't come up with a new one. That's the best way to start.

So again, write down the three things that you're grateful for, and those do not have to be related to work. This is important because your business, your online business, will always have ups and downs. The more it grows, the more stable it will be, but there will always be waves of ups and downs. If you connect your gratitude and your happiness to your business, your mood will also go up and down, and you don't want that to happen. You want to be grateful for the things you have, the relationships you have in your life, the house you have, the food you can eat, and the family you have. So be sure that the three things you're grateful for are not connected to work.

Then, think about the *two* things you've accomplished that you're proud of today because it's always easy to see exactly how much is left to achieve. It's always important to focus on two things you've already achieved. Look at the whole of what you've done so far.

And finally, think about *one* thing that you will do better tomorrow. This helps you to finish the work, and it's normal to think that work will never finish. Remember, when you think that you're not perfect, no one is perfect. Tell yourself you're going to do better tomorrow. That helps us put a stop to negative thoughts. You can choose one thing that you're going to do better tomorrow.

Again, these are the "three, two, ones":

- *Three* things you're grateful for unrelated to work.
- *Two* things that you are proud you accomplished today.
- *One* thing you will do better tomorrow.

This will help you to end the day correctly and to end your day effectively.

If you don't like where you are, then change your habits. Your habits determine your future.

The three things I gave you above, your non-negotiable, your powerful morning routine, how to end your day effectively, and the "mind movie" are some of the habits you can implement to change your life. They're going to help you become the new person you need to be to do the things you need to do to achieve the life, freedom, and income you want.

I want to help you implement this. As I said, this is a playbook. So it's not just something that you read, it's something that you need to implement, so you can achieve the freedom that you want. So on our website, www. zerotofreedomsecrets.com/freegifts, you will find our habit tracker.

The habit tracker is a tool I've designed to ensure that you can implement those three habits above to become that new person. It's free and a very easy template to use, so you can start tracking daily. When you do this consistently for the next 21 days, you will see how you are evolving into this new person. And part of the new, free, optimal you is *Productivity Power.*

STEP 3

Productivity Power

"Your time is limited, so don't waste it living someone else's life. Don't be trapped by dogma - which is living with the results of other people's thinking. Don't let the noise of other's opinions drown out your own inner voice" -Steve Jobs

The 64/4

Now let's talk about *productivity power*. I'm going to show you the five "Ps" of productivity power. I know there are a lot of Ps, right? But we're talking about productivity power and how to make sure that you're maximally productive so you can do in three hours a day what people generally need eight hours to accomplish. This is one of the ways to achieve maximum freedom.

First, let's eliminate the myth that you need to do many things to be productive because you don't.

I learned this when I launched my online business. I was still working a nine-to-five job, and my time was limited. I first had to focus on the main money needle mover, the things that would make money and make an impact. I couldn't focus on the little details because I didn't have the time, but that forced me to focus on what really mattered. To do this, I did something extreme.

You may be familiar with the Pareto principle. It's a rule that says that 80% of the assets come from 20% of the work, which in business means focusing on 20% of the tasks that will give you 80% of the result. It's more commonly referred to as the "80/20 rule."

But I decided to take that a step further by applying the 80/20 rule on the 80/20.

So focusing on 20% of the 20% (so 4%) tasks would give me 80% of the 80% (so 64%) results— that's the 64/4.

And I started applying that everywhere, focusing only on the 4% of the tasks that would give me 64% of the result. And I became super productive in my nine-to-five (which helped me get more and more free time until I quit), in my side hustle… in my life.

Well, when I say I had a nine-to-five job it was actually longer than that because I was working in one of the world's top digital marketing agencies (it was cool 😊). That meant I usually had to work extra hours because I was overpaid to make sure that we over-delivered to our over-paying clients.

Everything was "over."

But my new philosophy was that "less is more."

I was living in London, so working an extra hour or two and then trying to get back and forth from home to the office often took 40 minutes to an hour. So, in reality, that nine-to-five was more like eight-to-seven. *When would I have the time to actually grow my business?* This will sound absurd, but I grew my business by working between 5 a.m. to 8 a.m. every morning.

Again, this is the short-term sacrifice I had to make for my long-term success, which was not sustainable. I'll be the first to admit that.

But when I started working from 5-8 a.m. before going to my nine-to-five job, I knew it would only be for a couple of months because I was going to quit that job for my new business.

It depends on how long of a notice you want to give your current job. I recommend a one, two, or maximum of three months' notice because two or three months is enough to launch your online consulting business and start making a minimum of $5,000 per month. That's the minimum ($5k) because I have clients making 20, 30, or even 50k per month organically without spending a single cent on paid advertising.

We'll get to that later. For now, let's focus on the productivity power and how to make sure that those three hours are more effective than an eight-hour "day job."

Entering "the zone"

Let's talk about deep work. Deep work is when you're entering the zone. Have you ever been in that state where everything just flows? Where you can't be stopped, energy flows, ideas just come, and you're on a roll operating at your maximum performance level. That is called "in the zone."

I want to give you a very powerful strategy for entering the zone whenever you need it.

First, to enter the zone, you need to enter a specific state called "deep work." Deep work is defined as activities performed in a state of distraction-free concentration that pushes your cognitive abilities to their limits.

There are a few things that stand out. The first one is no interruption. And no interruption means you do not stop working. No one is physically interrupting you. No one is knocking on your door. Your phone is not ringing; it's turned off, out of sight, ideally in a separate room. This works really well, five to eight in the morning, because most of your friends, family, and roommates are sleeping. So it should be you looking at your computer and working with your mind.

The second thing is that there is a singularity of focus. Singularity of focus means you're only doing one thing. You're only doing that one thing, and you're only working on one task.

This is so important. Singularity of focus is like a laser. There is the sun which is super powerful. It's the strongest source of power we know. But because it's broad, it could be more effective in terms of power.

On the other hand, a laser is super effective with its power because its focus is on one point. This is the same with your energy. If you focus energy on different tasks, you're decreasing the energy that you're focusing on one single thing.

If you're multitasking, I recommend you stop. There is so much data out there that shows you that multitasking, in reality, is not productive. You're not effectively accomplishing multiple tasks; you're only switching from one task to another. And every time you switch from one task to another, you lose focus. This is very important to understand—focus on only one task.

This is non-negotiable because this is one of the secrets to working three hours a day to build your consulting freedom business making 5, 10, 20, 40, or 50k per month. When you focus only on three hours, that is all the work you will need to do in your own business.

So again, every single morning, I woke up at 5 a.m. and did three hours of work to create my online consulting business.

Before we get to the five Ps that will be the foundation of your business, I want to talk about another P—*procrastination.*

Procrastination comes from not knowing what you love. Think about it. When you do something that you love, you don't skip it. If you love going to the movies, you're not going to procrastinate. You're going to go because you love that. If you love pizza night with your best friend, you're not going to procrastinate because you love that. So the secret to avoiding procrastination is choosing to do what you love.

Identify your Superpower

When you do what you love, it doesn't feel like work. In fact, that is why in this book, we're going to talk about launching your freedom consulting business because this is one of the best business models for you to focus on doing exactly what you want. There are many business models out there to grow your freedom and your income, but most of them are missing the impact and the passion. Impact and passion are two fundamental things to ensure you love what you do. And it's a long-term thing.

For example, buying products from China and selling them on Amazon might give you sustainable revenue (we're talking about revenue and not profit), but in reality, who loves doing that? There is no passion.

There is no impact in buying low-quality products from China and reselling them on Amazon.

More importantly, the profit is so low when you do this that you will need a lot of sales to have a high income. I'm talking about having a consulting business making 10, 20, 50, 100k per month. I'm talking about a consulting freedom business with a 50% to 70% profit. Profit means money entering your bank.

With models like Amazon reselling, your profit can be 5% to 10%. So there is a huge difference there. But I don't want to talk about money here. I want to talk about the five Ps you can focus on when you're launching a consultant freedom business: *purpose, power, potential, passion,* and *problems.* Those are the only five Ps you need to understand to identify your superpower and to determine what kind of consulting business you should launch.

Let's start with the first—*Purpose.* And again, this is a playbook, so this is something where you should play with me. Ideally, I'm not the one telling you what type of consulting business you want to launch. I'm the one who asks you the right questions so you can find the right answers inside yourself.

Purpose

The first question to help understand your purpose is pretty simple. What is your purpose and vision for your online business? Purpose is the reason for the creation of the dream. A purpose precedes the plan. You must believe the vision is for victory before everybody has validation.

Everything starts in your mind. What is the purpose, the desire, and the vision for the consulting business you want to have?

For example, in my case, I want to help nine-to-fivers quit the job they hate so they can create a minimum of $12,000 per month with their freedom using our Secret Attraction Marketing strategies. This was my vision that became a reality two years ago, and we have already made more than a million dollars by helping other people live this reality.

My next question is, what have you seen in your industry, in your area of expertise, or influence that you can't stand anymore? What is the fire of frustration? This often creates tension and anger. For me, it's people losing a lot of money in paid advertising. I know this because, as I said, I was working in many top marketing agencies in London, and the reality was that some people lost a lot of money.

Obviously, some people made good money, but the reality is that with paid advertising, you're going to magnetically lose some budget when you're starting because there is a budget for testing, a budget for a margin of error. And I'm saying this very humbly because even working in London's top marketing agencies, they make mistakes. We're human; everyone makes mistakes.

The problem is that when you make mistakes in paid advertising, those mistakes cost money. And if you're starting out with your consulting business, you probably are using money from your savings that you worked very hard to earn.

I don't want you to risk your savings using paid advertising because it's very easy to lose. I help nine-to-fivers grow their business without using paid advertising.

The next question that will help you understand your purpose is thinking about what separates you from others. What are three things that make you stand out from your competition? You might be a fitness coach, for example. What makes you different from the other fitness coaches? You might be very good at design. What makes you different from other designers?

I have a client who is a really good friend who helps other friends get out of toxic relationships. We helped her create a program called Dump Your Toxic Relationship. Even if you're not a coach or you don't see yourself as a coach or consultant yet, start to think about what would be something that makes you different from others.

In my case, for example, it was the fact that I'm a digital nomad. This book is all about freedom of location, freedom of time, freedom in any terms, to be honest. The fact that I am a digital nomad and I have real marketing agency experience differentiates me from other gurus who don't have this real-life experience. They might be business coaches, but they don't travel, and they don't have the freedom I have.

To summarize, what is your purpose? What is something you've seen in the industry that you can't stand anymore? And what are the traits in it that make you stand out? You'll start to see your purpose, which is one of the five Ps.

Power

The next P is *power*. Understanding exactly what is your zone of genius. And if you're as humble as I am, you might not know this yet. It took me a lot of time to understand that I could help others. I didn't come up with this. One of my best friends told me this because he was working a nine-to-five job just like me, in a digital marketing agency just like me. He wanted to travel just like me, but he didn't have the power to make that leap. I've been coaching him for free to help him with this nine-to-five job. And he's the one who suggested to me that this was my power.

Same with my fiancé. When we met, she was working a nine-to-five job, but we both wanted to travel the world together, so I gave her all my support because that is my zone of genius. I realized that my zone of genius was helping people achieve the freedom they wanted. Guess what? That's also why I decided to write this book.

Now, list two things that make you happy and that you never outsource. Maybe it's two things you're already doing for free that you should be paid for.

Let me give you a good example. Gloria, who is now a health coach, was a food influencer for a very long time. She recommended to her friends how to have a healthy diet, how to become vegan without losing nutrients and muscle, and how to stay healthy using intuitive eating and herbal medicine. She had been doing that for free for many, many years.

For her, this didn't feel like working. That was her sort of genius; that was her power. So when she started to transform this power into a proper business, she started to grow her coaching freedom business to multiple six figures.

I want you to think about what is something that you're already doing that should be paid for, something that people need, and something that you love doing. If you don't know this yet, I challenge you to write two or three stories about turning points in your life. This will help you understand exactly what could be your zone of genius.

For me, it was when I looked at my boss five years ahead of me on the career ladder, and I saw that he wasn't happy. He didn't have any freedom.

He had three kids, a wife to satisfy, and lots of extra hours at work. He had no time, no passion, and no freedom.

That was my epiphany. And I remember that it prompted me to write a blog post:

Imagine yourself in five years doing exactly what you're doing right now. Are you happy, or are you unhappy? If you're happy seeing yourself in five years doing exactly what you're doing right now, then you're in a good place. Don't worry about that. What if, like me, when you see yourself five years down the road and imagine yourself doing the same thing, you feel horrified and depressed, and sad about the idea. It means that you need to quit.

That post went viral. I literally have people telling me, "Bruno, I want to quit," but they don't know how to do it. "Bruno, I really resonated with your words. This nine-to-five is a scam," and things like that. People were asking me how to deal with it. So that epiphany helped me understand that was *my* opinion—my zone of genius.

So try to write down two or three different moments in your life because that could help you build your zone of genius. And when you start to see your potential zone of genius, we can start to reverse engineer your superpower, what problems your ideal client has, and what amazing benefit you can help them achieve.

This is a moment of brainstorming for you. Brainstorm ways that your new idea can create an impact on people. Start imagining the exciting new product or service that aligns with what comes naturally to you, with your superpower. What feels good, and what can help you serve at a high level?

For me, it was helping ethical people with a strong passion and a strong expertise package this expertise in a coaching program and grow this coaching program to six figures while working from anywhere in the world. That's why it's called an online consulting freedom business.

Potential

The third P is *potential*. Now that you know your power and your *purpose*, you need to understand the *potential* of this.

If you look back over the last twelve months in your life, in your career, in your passion, in your business, what were the biggest needle movers?

For me, it's wanting a Two Comma Club award, an established award from using Clickfunnels to make at least $1 million on the platform.

I've traveled to eight countries in the last six months. When I say travel, I don't mean like a tourist for a few weeks, I mean literally living in those new places. I visually got this balance between the workplace and relationships. I'm very happy about the relationships that I have. About the freedom I have to play and dance, which is my biggest passion, while still being able to dedicate enough power to work to make sure my business is successful again.

Back to the three-hour habit, this balance helped me position myself as a business coach and differentiate myself from others. It's not just about business hustling, hustling, hustling, working, working, working, but more about finding that balance.

Let's think about what are the biggest needle movers for you. This is something that is really underestimated. Think about the biggest mistakes you've made in the past twelve months that would warn people of what not to do so they don't repeat it.

I love to say that your "mess" can become your "message."

Maybe you tried a certain diet, but it didn't work, so you can tell people to avoid it. Maybe you've been stuck in a bad relationship, and it took you a long time to understand how to exit that relationship, but now you can help others exit their bad relationship faster. Perhaps you were a smoker who learned the long-term, negative impact on your health. Now you can teach people how to stop smoking faster. I can go on forever.

There are so many ideas you can translate into a consulting business. It doesn't have to be big; you just have to focus. You have to solve a painful problem. Ideally, a painful problem you've navigated because your best clients will be the version of you from four to five years ago.

The same way that I was the version of me five years ago when I was working a nine-to-five, it took me five years to achieve my current status. With this playbook, you might do it in five months.

My mistake was investing a lot of money in advertising at the beginning. Because after I quit my job, I thought, *I have agency experience. I'm an expert with Google Ads and Facebook Ads.* So I just threw a lot of money into paid advertising, thinking I'd get a lot of clients. If only it were that easy.

I did this without doing the research. Without going through these five Ps, I immediately invested money in paid advertising, trying to get clients. I quickly created my own agency and invested money in Google advertising to find clients so I could use my Google Ads skills to make them more money.

Guess what? I lost a lot of money. Not because I wasn't good at advertising. Remember, that was my job. I learned from the best Google

Ads agency. But because of my impatience and because I didn't have a guide to show me the way, I skipped many important steps—doing the research properly, having your social proof, understanding my superpower, and what my passion was.

Because Google Ads was really my passion, I didn't do this right. I was doing it for work, but I needed to do it for myself, and I failed miserably. I lost so much money that I had to temporarily get another nine-to-five job. I don't want you to make the same mistake. I'm happy that you're reading this book.

Passion

The fourth P is *passion*. Since you're choosing the type of business you want to launch, you might as well choose a business you love, right? A business that you're passionate about, and this is easy for you to find out. Take three to five power and passion topics you could talk about for 10-15 minutes easily and passionately. Those are the things you can teach and share with the world.

If you want my example, my topic number one was "quitting a nine-to-five." In order to quit the nine-to-five, I read a lot of books (in fact, this book you're reading is a fantastic summary of the best books out there which talk about living life on your terms.)

I really think that society cannot brainwash us to feel that we need to identify. And the fact that the pension should be the final reward when you're 60 years old, and then you can finally develop a lack of freedom. And that, for me, was probably a scam because the reality is that right now is the best time to be happy, not when you're 60. Right now is the time to have a mini pension, as I call it, where you just close the business, go wherever you want, and enjoy your life.

Obviously, my topic number two was digital nomad because that is literally who I am.

And my third topic was turning a passion into a profession. Because every time my friends were telling me they didn't have a skill that could become a business, I always said, "Yes, you do." You just need to look deeper.

So what are the three topics that you could talk about forever? And if you need help finding those three topics, ask your friends. Ask your best friend. Look at your computer browser. What kind of research do you do on Google or YouTube?

Think about your favorite movie. Because one thing that I realized is that you choose your mind movie because you see yourself as the protagonist. So you somehow relate a lot to that protagonist with a superpower.

So when you choose your favorite movie, you can really relate to that protagonist.

Problems

The last P is *problems*. Now that you know your *purpose, power, potential,* and *passion*, it's time to understand the problem you're going to fix, and what problems you can confidently solve. And don't worry if you can't solve that problem confidently. For now, you can learn how to do it. Remember, you still have a couple of months. In a couple of months, you can learn everything.

Make a list of three to five problems you can solve with your passion, potential, power, and focus. Ask yourself how painful that problem is—

the biggest pain, the biggest paycheck. Now we're starting to get into the marketing part. People pay to solve pains. So think about a big pain you can solve because people pay for two reasons.

The first reason is that they want to get closer to a desire, like making a certain amount of money.

The second reason is that they want to get away from pain, like quitting their nine-to-five.

So guess what? I could focus on helping people make more money, which is a desire, or I can focus on helping them eliminate their nine-to-five, which is the pain.

Which one of those two people will be more motivated to invest?

Exactly! Solve the pain. Because even if people want to achieve a desire, there's still some work that needs to be done, and there is still some effort. So even if someone really wants that desire, they might procrastinate and not do the work. When there is a big pain, people urgently need to fix it, and they pay the person who can help them fix it.

So for the three or five problems you listed, think about how painful it is on a scale of one to ten. Next, think about how much you would enjoy solving that problem, again on a scale of one to ten, where one is you wouldn't enjoy it at all, and ten is you would enjoy it a lot.

Finally, think about how confident you are that you are able to deliver that transformation from one to ten:

- **One to Three** - you learn it. You're not super confident, not super ready, but you're learning.

- **Three to Six** - you've already done it for yourself. So if you're helping people to quit smoking, the fact that you've already stopped smoking yourself, you can give some good advice.

- **Six to Ten** - you're already doing it with others. You've already helped your friends stop smoking.

So with those three categories, you should have a range of numbers.

And when you sell this rate, then you're going to have a total rate between these problems. You're going to have three to five problems with a rate that goes from zero to 30. So look at the one with the highest rate and pick one.

If you want our free "Superpower Finder," go to
www.zerotofreedomsecrets.com/freegifts.

You've chosen your problem at this point. You have your *purpose*, your *power*, your *potential*, your *passion*, and the *problems* that you're solving.

Now you're ready to create your *Magnetic Offer*.

STEP 4
Create Your Magnetic Offer

"If you have a business and you're struggling financially,
the solution is simple: Make More Offers."
-Myron Golden

The riches in the niches

Let's talk about magnetic offers by telling you the story of Mark and Odette Clayton, a fantastic couple from Manchester, United Kingdom.

When I started working with Odette and Mark, I immediately realized that I was working with a fantastic couple with a fantastic service who had no idea what a "magnetic offer" was.

They used to sell a very low ticket offer. By "low-ticket," I mean anything that costs between $10 to $1,000.

They used to sell a general course with tips for couples, and every now and then, they were doing couples therapy for $99.

So I first asked them, "Do you think your offer is magnetic?"

And I remember them saying, "What do you mean by magnetic?"

So I told them exactly what a magnetic offer is. But instead of just telling them, I showed them by asking questions about their couple's therapy:

Who are those couples specifically?

Are they already married?

Are they about to get married?

Are they about to divorce?

Are they Christian?

Are they from another religion?

We started understanding exactly who the people that they wanted to help were. Couples who wanted to feel more passionate about each other.

So we created a program called Couple Revitalization, which helped us increase their course from $99 to $400.

We were able to raise the price because it was more specific.

And we decided to get even more specific. In fact, what I do is exactly that: I help people to understand who their dream clients are, what is their superpower, and sell high ticket programs between $1,000 to $21,000.

We narrowed it down to who the specific couple they can help and what specific problem that couple is struggling with.

We realized that Odette and Clayton they're very religious. They are a fantastic Christian couple who live only by the Bible. So we decided to create a program specifically for other couples like that and for other Christian married couples on the verge of divorce.

Do you know how much divorce costs? It's at least $50,000, and this is only if you consider the financial damage.

Think about the emotional damage, the children involved, and a long legal battle; it's damaging in so many ways.

If Odette and Clay can save a couple's marriage for a $2,000 fee, in reality, not only is that couple saving $48,000 in divorce but also staying with the love of their life, having that romantic dream, with a good family relationship and not having any family drama.

When you process all this, it's easy to see that the $19 program they were selling is actually worth $50.000, so I helped them to raise their price to $1,997 instead because they narrowed it down and they had a "magnetic offer."

The new magnetic offer was, *We help Christian couples revitalize their marriage and avoid divorce.*

Can you see how powerful this is?

Can you see how it talks exactly to a big problem?—Christian couple divorce.

So if I'm part of a Christian couple and I want to live by the Bible and my marriage is on the verge of a divorce, I will think, "Wow, Odette and Clay are the perfect coaches because they are Christian just like me so we're aligned in term of relationship values and they could help me save my marriage"

Their offer is to "revitalize a marriage," which is their client's desire/need, and "avoid divorce," which is the big pain they want to avoid.

And now the same course, literally the same course that was "Tips for Couples" at $19, is now a magnetic offer worth $1,997 because they're talking to a specific audience with a very specific problem, giving a very specific solution.

Those are the elements to make your offer MAGNETIC. The more specific, the more magnetic.

Alignment

Now, let's break down how you can create your magnetic offer. Remember before when we worked on the five Ps of productivity power? Understanding what is the purpose, power, potential, passion, and problems that you can solve? Perfect.

Now that you've listed those problems, the only thing that you need to do is create a solution for those problems. And if you want to do an extra step, I highly recommend you think about the most painful, or the biggest problem you can solve.

All right, so what you want to do when you create the list of problems you can solve is turn those problems into a solution.

That is what an offer is, a solution to a problem. Literally, that's it.

And when you make that offer to someone, you're inviting them to join you in solving the problem.

When you make this switch, you realize that making an offer is not something "pushy," "salesy," or "needy."

It is quite the opposite.

When you don't make an offer to a potential person who you can help, you're doing a disservice to the other person (and potentially an entire community you can help).

The consulting business is all about servicing, and that's why it is my favorite model. In fact, I don't sell, I serve.

Here's an example:

If I'm a health coach or a fitness coach, and I help people get fit through a diet, one of the problems my clients might have is buying food at the store.

"Grocery shopping is hard and confusing. I won't like it, and I will suck at it." That is the problem that your potential customers might have.

So the solution, which is the offer I can make, is "how to make buying healthy food easy and enjoyable so that anyone can do it, especially busy moms."

Again, have you seen how I niche down here with busy moms?

Another problem for my potential clients is that "It takes so much time to buy healthy food and do the grocery shopping."

My solution might be "How to buy healthy food quickly."

And I can come up with a list where it makes it easier and faster for them to shop.

I can help them buy recurring orders on Amazon or any online grocery service. I can help them make a shopping list. I can help them add the list once to their cart to have the food delivered to their place, and it can be set to a recurring delivery schedule if they wish. So I just came up with a solution that saves them time, gives them healthy ingredients every week, and helps them to stay fit.

That's a good offer that solves a specific problem.

If the problem is, "If I travel, I won't know what to eat." My solution can be how to get healthy food when traveling.

If you made me that offer, for example, I would buy it because I travel a lot and one of my problems is having healthy food while I travel.

And I'd be happy to pay you a lot because I have the "problem" of traveling so much and even if I'm generally pretty fit thanks to my victory hour routine, sometimes I put on some weight because I struggle to eat healthy in some countries.

So if you have an offer to solve this problem and you're not making me an offer, you're doing a disservice to me. :)

You see how those examples work because they talk about specific solutions?

The more specific, the better.

And at this stage, the only thing you do is understand the specific problems you can solve based on the exercise we've done before for a specific audience that you would love to work with.

Your mission statement

So now, it's time for you to be creative. Think about any niche in health, wealth, relationship, or personal development and try to "niche down," narrow it down to a specific problem you can solve for a specific person.

If I'm a fitness coach, just because I want to keep going with this example, instead of saying I help people get fit, I could niche down to say I help busy women to get a flat belly. I can niche down even more to say I help busy moms to have fast and easy healthy meals and to get back their pre-pregnancy body shape.

Can you see how I niche down from working with people to working with women, which is cutting the niche in half, and working with moms, which is a sub-niche of women? So the more niche you get, the more specific it is.

Now, if a busy mom reads my offer, she will say, "Yes, this offer is specifically designed for me because I'm not a 20-year-old with plenty of time to shop, with a fast metabolism, and all this time to work out. I'm a busy woman who just came out from pregnancy, and I want to lose weight fast, and I don't have a lot of spare time." So their offer needs to be personalized. That's why when you niche down, your offer will sound irresistible and magnetic for that specific offer.

As I told you before, with Odette and Mark's story, they managed to massively increase their fee. They increased the price of their Tips for Couples course from $19 to $1,997, selling a program that helps Christian couples revitalize their marriage and avoid divorce. Literally, the same product, a hundred times the price. This is the power niching down to a specific problem for a specific niche. So at this point, you should have a specific problem you're solving and the specific niche you're targeting.

And you can put together your mission statement which is:

I help a unique niche solve a specific problem in a unique way that reverses their biggest objection.

Now replace the statement below with your findings:

I help (specific niche) achieve/do/solve (specific desire they have or problem you're solving) with/without (the thing they want/the thing they don't want)

For example, my mission: I help nine-to-fivers break free and achieve their definition of freedom without wasting money, energy and time.

Gloria's example is: *I help busy women to lose weight for good without diets.*

Now it's your turn; what's your mission statement?

Write it down.

Because when you decide to write down your mission statement, you can start creating your high ticket magnetic offer.

Why a high ticket offer?

Let's talk about why it should be a high ticket offer, why it should be an offer that costs $1,000, $10,000, $50,000, or $100,000. I recommend you start with something between $1,000 to $5,000. This is because the more people pay for your program, the more effort they will put into implementing the work.

Have you ever bought one of those PDFs online in which, for $20, you get five secret exercises that will give you a six-pack before summer? I don't know about you, but I used to buy those things. But because I wasn't really invested, I never read any of them. I have never done the exercises, and I just stopped. Did that ever happen to you? It happened to a lot of people.

Now, imagine you pay $5,000 to join an online fitness group, and the trainer gives you the exercises, and there are also calls from the trainer a couple of times a week to check on your progress. It keeps you accountable. You have a group that motivates you to keep working out. You see other people in the group getting results, and you don't want to fall behind, so you do the workouts too. Can you see the difference between the two?

I did see the difference when I bought my *$90* PDF to get my six-pack back before summer four years ago. I did the exercises for a day then I stopped following the pdf.

But when I wanted to step it up, I invested in an online personal coach paying $3,499. He gave me exercises to follow, but to be honest with you, the exercise was very similar to the $19 PDF I bought four years ago.

So what was the difference? I was financially invested in this, and because I had a coach who was keeping me accountable and motivated to make a change, I got the results, and I got fitter than ever.

Did something like this ever happen to you?

This is the power of high ticket. When people invest in high ticket, you will obviously get more profit. But the most important thing is that you can focus on a small number of clients. If your freedom number is $10k per month and you're selling your program at $5k per month, you would only need two clients each month.

You can focus all your time and energy on those two clients, use this money to improve your skills to become a better fitness coach, and maybe invest in a certification to become a certified personal trainer or invest in other apps, tools, software, educational books that can help you to become better at what you do.

That's why high ticket is always better.

And finally, this is very subtle, but when people invest in high ticket, they perceive it as high value.

Here's an example, and is a proven exercise.

In a restaurant with 10 people were given three bottles of wine: one low price, one medium price, and one high price. The low-price bottle rated poorly, the average-priced bottle rated better, but the high-priced bottle was by far rated as the best.

But guess what? They were all the same wine! Because you paid more, you perceive a higher value. And that is the same for anything that you buy. When you pay a premium price, you perceive premium value.

And in the case of a consulting program, you will see the service and the person you work with as a premium value (unless the content or the person are objectively of low value).

This will work for you as well. If someone invests in you, they will start seeing you as having higher value, listen more intently to the information you give them, and implement it more.

So start charging premium high tickets and also start investing in premium high tickets because if you're not "practicing what you preach," there's going to be an internal conflict when you need to ask for a premium high ticket price to clients who want to work with you.

So start investing in premium high ticket offers so you can start getting premium high ticket clients and deliver your premium high ticket magnetic offer.

Magnetic Offer Delivery

You have your mission offer, we've discussed the price, and we've also discussed how to turn problems into a solution.

Now, let's discuss the delivery.

There are different ways that you can choose to deliver your magnetic offer. Here are the three most effective: done-*for*-you, done-*with*-you, and do-it-*yourself*.

There is a fulfillment commitment to keep in mind with each one of these. The done-*for*-you are the easiest to sell but the hardest to fulfill because you are literally doing the work for someone else.

Imagine that you're a marketing agency, and you're helping people to make more money with Google advertising. That means that you are doing all the work, doing the keyword research, creating the ad copy, actually doing the Google ad strategy, monitoring all the progress, and sending a report at the end of each day.

The done-*for*-you are the easiest to sell because there's not too much client commitment other than investing the money. Someone is giving you money and expecting you to do it for them.

The hardest to sell is do-it-*yourself* because people don't like to do the work. Have you noticed? A lot of people don't want to work.

So if you send a guide for them to do the work themselves, they will be skeptical that they can realistically complete it properly—that's a hard sell. It's easy to fulfill because you just have to send your report, your course, or whatever, and they do it themselves.

The sweet spot is in the middle. They do it *with* you.

This is the model that has been booming in the last couple of years, especially after Covid. In this model, you are a consultant, and you don't have to put too much time and energy into doing all the work for them (hence why you get the time freedom), but at the same time, for them, it's not too scary because they have your guidance and don't have to do it themselves.

From your point of view, it's easy because you can give them guides, books, and personalized consultation through calls, and you can also add more people if you decide to do group sessions.

Let's talk more about the best ways to fulfill the done-*with*-you service.

First, if you've never done anything like this, you want to start with a done-*for*-you model where you are doing all the work. This is important because if you're just starting out, you need to learn exactly how to help them, and you're learning even better how to do the work.

When you've done a few done-*for*-you services, then you can move to the done-*with*-you service, where you do it with them. You give them some guides, books, recordings, and lessons on how to do it, and you work with them to get the most out of the material.

If you then want to scale, you can package all those tools you're providing in the done-*with*-you offer into a do-it-*yourself* product. At this point, you've become really good at creating those guides, and you can just sell the guides.

Now let's talk about how you want to deliver it. There are many different ways to deliver this kind of service. After you list the problem and the solutions, you also need to list all the ways you could solve that problem. And again, use a cheat code to make it easier to think through. You can get this cheat code on my website

www.zerotofreedomsecrets.com/freegifts.

Let's go back to the example that "buying healthy food is hard, confusing, expensive, and time-consuming." I could provide a one-on-one solution, like texting clients while they are at the store and teaching them how to shop.

I could provide a personalized grocery list. I could do a full-service shopping option, where I buy their food and drop it at their house.

We're talking 100% done for them.

Those are just some examples of how to offer a one-on-one solution. If I wanted to provide a small group solution, I might offer in-person grocery shopping where I meet a bunch of clients and take them shopping.

I could help the group make their weekly grocery list, and I could do this once or weekly. I could buy their food and have it delivered to them.

How about a one-to-many solution where I take the group to a store so they can follow me around as I shop and ask questions?

You could also record that tour and provide it to future clients. Again, you can find the cheat code on our website

www.zerotofreedomsecrets.com/freegifts.

You can choose the how: one-to-one, small group, or one-to-many.

You can choose the way you want to present it: done-*for*-you, done-*with*-you, or do-it-*yourself.*

You can choose what kind of support you want to give, if it's in person, on WhatsApp, or via Zoom calls.

And you want to choose how they consume it: video, in writing, etc.

And you can choose the opening times: If that is from nine-to-five. If that is Monday to Friday. If that's only Monday, Tuesday, and Thursday (like I do).

You have the complete freedom to choose how you want to build your offer around your lifestyle, instead of building your lifestyle around your work.

So you put together all the problems you mentioned before, put together all the solutions, and put together the way you present it.

Finally, let's use the example of my client's relationship coach I mentioned earlier.

They help Christian couples revitalize their marriage and avoid divorce, which is the magnetic offer.

The way I help them to build their magnetic offer to have financial, location, and time freedom is with a "one-to-many" session. So instead of having one-on-one sessions, they mainly do group calls.

They have one group call for men and another group call for women. They do this because, in reality, most couples have the same problem.

So when they have group calls, this is powerful because someone in the group could ask a question that someone else hasn't thought about yet.

So everybody grows faster.

In this case, in the group calls, they're all married Christian men/women who want to revitalize their marriage and avoid divorce. Guess what? They're going to have most of the same problems. So when my client has a group of men overcome their problem, those people have a massive "group collective benefit."

Because when a man asks a question and the coach gives the solution, the other people there may not think about asking that question but will have the solution they need.

That is why group sessions are so powerful.

So, as soon as you get your first three or four clients, I recommend you move to group sessions.

Let's get back to how to put everything together.

You put together the problem with the solution and how you're going to offer it. If it's a done-*with*-you or do-it-*yourself*, one-to-one group session, or small group session. When you put all these things together, you should have your magnetic offer.

To summarize, make sure that your offer is magnetic.

The more specific, the more attractive.

You don't want to have a broad niche because "riches are in the niches."

You have a specific painful problem that you're solving.

You created a specific solution to solve that problem, you know a specific way to solve it, and you have a specific way of delivering it to people.

Now that you have a magnetic offer, you can focus on creating training data to help people become the person they need to become to do the things they need to do to have the thing they need to have.

Trainings That Transform

To create trainings that transform, there is a very specific and simple process. Think about the transformation you want to deliver to your clients. There's point A, where they are right now, and point B, which is where they want to be. You want to break down a journey from point A to point B. Let's go back to the fitness coach example.

If you are a fitness trainer and you help busy moms lose weight, what is the first thing they need to do to lose 10 lbs in 3 months?

Again, considering that point A is where they are right now.

They are super busy and overweight and don't have time to cook healthy meals and exercise.

Point B is the desired situation, where they're fit, confident, optimize their time, and live a happy life.

How do they go from point A to point B?

Let's break it down into four steps.

1. **Mindset:** The mindset is always the first step. Remember that I told you about the 80/20 rule? We always start with mindset because mindset is always 80%. In this case, I will create a mindset program where I have busy moms rewire their brains, understanding that they *can* find the time because time for health

is important. And if they're healthy, the baby is going to be healthy. So that is the first step.

2. **Do the grocery shopping quickly:** I explain, for example, how to optimize and organize their grocery list. They can either shop on one day or have all their groceries delivered weekly on a Monday, so they don't have to go to the store. I will show them how to make quick meals that don't require a lot of time to make.

3. **Exercise:** Having a consistent exercise routine is hard, especially after having a baby. Going to the gym is not always an option when you have a new life that requires full-time attention. Instead of going to the gym, they can work out from home, using their baby as a weight, literally weightlifting their baby, holding them as they do squats, or putting them on their back while they're doing push-ups, for example. I'm just being creative, but you can figure that out.

4. **Maintain your body:** How to stick to a diet and how to make it a habit, and work out even when you don't feel like it.

Those are the four steps that will help her go from her point A to point B.

I have a story about one of my clients, Sahil. He is an electrician who made $100,000 per month organically. His point A was "electrician coming from India." And his point B was "being a family guy who makes $100,000 per month to provide for his wife, future kids, and her parents." Here are his five steps.

1. **Optimal You:** Sahil's first step was the *optimal you,* becoming someone who can achieve that result.

2. **Productivity power:** He still needed to do his nine-to-five job while building this new business around his passion.

3. **Creating the magnetic offer:** Making sure the offer was so magnetic that people didn't want to say no.

4. **Optimizing client acquisition:** How to optimize getting clients, which is exactly what we will talk about in the next step.

5. **Automate growth:** How to automate this growth. Because at some point, if you want to keep growing and keep having that freedom, which is the main objective here, you have to automate what you're doing.

6. **Selling through serving:** If you make a lot of money, you have that freedom, but if you're not fulfilled by impacting more people, you will not be happy. There are so many stories of successful people who killed themselves because they were depressed. Even if they were rich and had a family around them, they had everything that you could dream of, but they were depressed. This happens when you spend all your time making everyone happy and not taking time for yourself. That's why you must be able to create impact. And the way that I teach impact is by selling through serving.

We'll talk more about this in the next two steps. But first, let's talk about the optimization secrets. I'm going to tell you exactly how to go from selling your $1,000 offer to make $128k per month to month.

STEP 5

Secret Attraction Marketing

"When you want something, all the universe conspires in helping you to achieve it." -Paulo Coelho, The Alchemist

The hybrid model.

In this step, I'm going to show you how to grow your business using Secret Attraction Marketing.

First, let me tell you a story. When I was little, around ten years old, we were playing this game in Italy called the Game of the Bottle (spin the bottle in the U.S.). I'm sure most reading this have either heard of it or played some version of it as a young person. It was a very stupid game where you make a small circle, alternating boy and girl. There's a bottle in the middle, and each person takes a turn spinning the bottle on its side until it points to someone in the circle. By rule, you are supposed to kiss that person.

So, getting back to my story. All the girls there were afraid of being chosen because they didn't want to get kissed by my huge lips, thinking they would suffocate or something like that. Now that I think about it, it was very stupid, to be honest. But for some reason, this stuck in my head for a very long time, and I didn't feel attractive for very long. I decided to do everything in my power to become more attractive. I decided to work out not just my body but also my brain. I decided to read a lot to become more interesting. I traveled a lot to open my mind. I grew my dreadlocks and learned how to dance.

All of those things, to be honest, started because I wanted to attract the right person. But when I started marketing, I realized that attraction works in anything, in life, in flirting, and in business. So I didn't like the idea of the cold DM, meaning sending cold messages to people you don't know yet. There is also the cold email or cold calling to people whose names you get from a list. That's even worse because I'm an introvert, so there was no way I could call a potential client who didn't know me yet, try to make friends with them, and then try to sell them. This was not going to work for me.

So I started to apply the same attraction principle in business and marketing. I was going to attract the right client instead of chasing them. Before you think this could be a lame strategy, let me tell you exactly what I mean by *Secret Attraction Marketing*.

First of all, if you want to grow your business, there are really two methods. You can either go outbound, meaning that you send messages, calls, or emails to your relevant potential clients, or you can go inbound by sharing content and pulling people to you.

If we go back to attraction marketing, I prefer a hybrid approach, a bit of a mix between the two, because if you only do cold call or outbound Marketing, you'd be like that guy who just approached every girl at the bar with a shitty pickup line (I apologize to our female readers, but hopefully you can relate with this analogy). Sure, one out of 100 girls will say yes, but that is a terribly inefficient numbers game you don't want to play.

However, if you do only content and inbound marketing, you'd be like that good-looking dude who just sits there and waits for women to approach him. But guess what? Even if you're attractive and people want to meet you, if you just passively wait for others to take the initiative, you'll be waiting a long time. And the sad thing is, maybe those people are thinking in their heads, *That guy is really cool. I hope he says hi*, and "cool dude" will never know. We need to find a middle ground.

The attraction marketing hybrid model is what works best. This is when you share content on your chosen organic channel, wait for people to engage with that content, and then proactively reach out to all of them.

I have some examples on my social media profile. If you follow me on Facebook, for example, Bruno Cine Morris, you will see exactly what I mean from the first post you'll see in my profile. You will see comments from people who said: "*Yes, I want this. I want this thing that you're offering. I'm interested in your mindset. I'm inspired by your content.*"

This makes it super easy to start a conversation with them and push them to the next step, whether it's a call, a strategy session, or sending people to buy your book, your free or low-ticket course.

This is what I call Secret Attraction Marketing, where it's a hybrid model between the DM sending the first message and the inbound of content creation. I always believe that a mix works.

Now that we've talked about Secret Attraction Marketing, let's learn how you can grow your business.

Four Moves to $128k per month

Specifically, you'll discover how to scale a business from $10,000 per month to $128,000 per month with only four moves, and you can add or remove zeros to the formulas, and it still applies. Do you think you can remember four moves?

Before I tell you what those moves are, I want you to know something. Every business growth coach and consultant teaches the same four moves. Russell Brunson teaches the same four moves that I do. Myron Golden teaches the same moves. Frank Kern teaches the same four moves, and so does Tony Robbins. That's because there are only four moves when it comes to growing and scaling businesses. If you have a business that you would like to scale, then you must make these four moves. When you figure out how to effectively activate this hyper-growth business strategy, your business will grow exponentially. Are you ready for the four business moves?

They are *lead generation*, *lead conversion*, *customer ascension*, and *customer retention*.

Let's dig into them one at a time, then put them together and watch what happens next. To keep the math simple, we'll use small, even numbers. Keep in mind, though, that it doesn't matter what the numbers are. The principles still apply. First, you need to look at what action you're taking to consistently hit your monthly revenue number.

Next, you need to find out what you're doing that's keeping you stuck at that number. Let's assume that you have a core product offer. Let's call it CPO for simplicity of $1,000, which, again, if you're starting out, you're probably going to want to start around $1,000. So every time you make a

ZERO TO FREEDOM SECRETS

sale, you are making $1,000. If your business is doing $10,000 per month in revenue, you're generating ten sales per month, which is a couple of weekly sales—very achievable. To generate those sales, you first have to generate leads, right? So let's say that you're generating 100 leads per month. And let's assume that you have a 10% conversion rate. 10% of 100 gets you ten sales per month. Get the picture? Good.

Now, let's scale your business by more than 10x. How do we do that using only four moves?

Move 1

Move number one is *lead generation*. The first move you need to make is to increase the number of leads you generate. If you double your number of leads from 100 to 200 and everything else stays the same, then you just doubled your business revenue and profit. You only made one of the four moves, and you already doubled your business. Can you see the magic and the power of this? We're just getting started. In other words, you fix one thing, but you're making twice as much. Instead of making $10,000 per month, you're now making $20,000 per month. Double your revenue by doubling your leads.

You're probably thinking, *That sounds great, Bruno, but how do I do that?*

Have you ever heard of a lead magnet? A lead magnet is something that is really attractive to your clients. So when you create a lead magnet and you add this component to your business, you could potentially double the leads at a mind-blowing level.

Do you know how many businesses and people around the world don't know what a lead magnet is? If you want to become a business growth coach or consultant, for example, you can make a fortune just by teaching business owners how to capture leads using lead magnets. In fact, you could build an opt-in funnel for a business owner and have them pay you for the leads. After the business owner gets the leads, it's up to them to convert those leads into paying customers. That is not hard stuff; it's actually pretty easy. It's one of the things we teach at www.zerotofreedomsecrets.com, in case you want to see more details on lead generation.

Move 2

Now, this is where the magic starts to happen–*lead conversion.*

The next thing you do to grow your business is to improve your lead conversion process. You improve your lead conversion by improving your sales process. The sales process that I teach will enable you to work *with* human nature instead of working *against* it. When you work with human nature, it works *for* you. When you work against human nature, it works *against* you, which, by the way, is a battle you can't win.

Let's start with what my business coach calls "psychological art history." This is the art of painting word pictures and hanging them in the minds of your prospect to have them see the world in a whole new light. You'll see a lot of examples of this throughout this book if you're looking for them. Along with psychological artistry, my sales framework relies heavily on emotional cooperation and logical justification. When you use emotional cooperation in selling, you create an environment that makes your prospect feel like buying with logical justification; you're supporting that feeling with a logical reason to buy. You've got to make your prospect feel like buying.

Again, you might be thinking, *Bruno, that sounds great, but how do I do that?*

Good question. You can reach emotional cooperation by using what Russell Brunson called the "big domino" and "the three secrets." The "big domino" is the main thing you have to get people to believe for them to say yes to your offer. "The three secrets" are what Russell uses to break old beliefs that would stop them from taking on the new belief, causing them to say yes to your offer.

In a nutshell, "the three secrets" are:

1. Change their *primary* limiting beliefs about your offer.
2. Change their *external* limiting beliefs about your offer.
3. Change their *internal* limiting beliefs about your offer.

Most people don't know about the "big domino" and "the three secrets." And I'm not going to go into detail about it in this book, but it's all laid out in Russell Brunson's *Expert Secrets* book. If you haven't already read *Expert Secrets*, buy it because it's really powerful if you do what it says. If you want the link, you can find it on

www.zerotofreedomsecrets.com/freegifts.

If you use any of our lead magnet framework to convert more sales, you could easily double your conversion rate. If you go from 10% conversion rate to 20% conversion, you've just doubled your revenue.

Again, think about it. You just doubled your lead generation from 100 leads per month to 200 leads per month. Then you double your conversion from 10% to 20%. Since 20% of 200 is 40, you are now making 40 sales per month with your $1,000 product.

Wait a minute! Did you just see what happened? We only made two moves! We doubled your leads from 100 to 200. Then we doubled your conversion from 10% to 20% (assuming your leads stayed the same and you were improving your conversions). If you were at $10,000 a month with a $1,000 core offer, you scale to $20,000 a month with the first move and to $40,000 with the next move. You quadrupled your business by only making two moves!

Move 3

Move number three—*customer ascension*. This term "move" isn't about leads, it's about customers and clients. That's because once you generate leads and convert them into buyers, those prospects are no longer leads—they're customers. They've converted or transformed into your client base. Now it's time to level them up.

Customer ascension simply means you're going to add a premium value offer to your mix. Most people who understand this concept call it a high ticket offer. I like to describe it based on what the client gets from the encounter more than what I get. That's why I use the term "premium value offer" instead of "high ticket offer."

Let's say you create a $10,000 premium value offer, and to make it simple, we'll call it PVO. And your offer is to all of the people who bought your $1,000 core product, the C people, we'll call them. For the sake of this illustration, let's say you convert 10% of those buyers to also take advantage of your PVO.

Since 10% of 40 sales per month is four and four times $10,000 is $40,000, you just added an extra $40,000 per month to your revenue.

This is probably my favorite move. If you add this $40,000 to the $40,000 per month you had by doubling down the number of leads and conversion rate, you are now $80,000 per month. If you don't already have a PVO, pay special attention to this next session. You need to understand something that most people get backward. One of the most important things that I do for my clients, one of the most valuable things I do for them is charge a premium to work with me.

You might be wondering, *Bruno, don't you do that for yourself?*

No, because I don't need their money anymore. But they need to pay me. Why? Because you sell like you buy. People who are unwilling to pay will be unable to charge.

If you desire to sell a premium value offer, you must be a buyer of premium value offers. It's a right of passage. People who want to sell premium value offers but have never bought a premium value offer will have too much internal conflict and are deceiving not only themselves but also their prospects. They think they will be able to help someone cross over into the world of premium value offers, but they have never crossed over themselves. They don't even really believe in the process.

When I sell somebody a PVO, I'm freeing them to sell somebody else a PVO because now they know people are willing to pay $10,000, $20,000, $50,000, or even $100,000. Why? Because *they* just did. If you buy a $50,000 program, you're not going to have a hard time charging somebody $10,000. The limitations that you have are in your mind. All you need to say is, "This is how much it is to work with me. I charge $10,000. Do you want to pay me that upfront or in two or three payments?" You do that for ten potential clients a month, and you will make more than a million dollars a year from now.

When you stop putting more faith in your limitations than you do in your leverage, you will begin to experience a life of flow or a life of financial freedom.

I'm going to tell you what I know for a fact to be true. You don't have to take my word for it. I will recommend that you do your own research. But I know beyond any shadow of a doubt that the master key to success in any achievement is to take ownership of the result before you know the fact.

Stop thinking, *As soon as I know how to do it, I'm going to do it.*

Start thinking, *I'm going to do it, and figure it out while I'm doing it.*

Don't say, "I'll do it as soon as I learn how," because you don't get to start learning "how" until you start doing it. The master key to having a quantum leap is to start to leap before you know how you're going to land. Take ownership of the result before you know the path.

At this point, we've made only three of the four moves to grow a business. We've doubled the number of leads and doubled the conversion numbers. For the buyers of CPO, we've added a PVO with a 10% conversion rate. That means we've taken your business from $10,000 to $80,000 a month. That's $960,000 per year! You haven't even made the last move yet, and you're already a millionaire making $80,000 per month.

Do you follow this? Can you start seeing your financial freedom already?

Move 4

What's the last move? Move four is *customer retention*. You've got to improve your retention to keep your freedom. But how do you do that?

We improve retention through continuity. Continuity means you set the product once but get paid for it every year, every month, or every week. Several kinds of products work well for continuity, like newsletters, SaaS (Software as a service-a way of delivering applications over the internet as a service), membership, etc. One of my favorite continuity models is a Forced Continuity Offer or FCO.

Let's say, for example, that you sell a course or coaching program, teaching someone to do something that they already want to learn how to do. But you teach them how to do it by using software that makes that task easier.

For example, I help people to get more clients using organic marketing, and I also give them a software that helps them to automate this process, so they don't need to do the manual work of finding the people or the group, adding them as a friend, attracting them with content, and sending a message. Most of this process can be completely automated with the software that I recommend. What you do is give them a 14 or 30-day trial of the software. Then, once they understand the value of it and are used to using it, you start charging for the use of that software.

Here's the easy math:

Let's say you add a $100 per month Subscription offer to make your $1,000 CPO. You could even make it mandatory. If someone wants to purchase your CPO, they must also purchase your subscription offer, ideally after a free trial. At 40 sales per month, that's a total of 480 sales at the end of the year. If you multiply those 480 sales times the first continuity purchase for $100 per month, that's $48,000 per month. When you add the $48,000 per month from the FCO to the $40,000 per month from the PVO added to the $40,000 per month from the CPO, that's a total of $128,000 per month in four freedom moves. Do you see how easy that was? You literally achieve your financial freedom with four moves.

When you make your offer, you have to keep in mind that you are not the result, and you don't produce the result for clients. You sell the outcome, and the process produces the result.

Now, you might be asking yourself, *Bruno, how do I sell the outcome?*

Well, I'm glad you asked. My presentation is simple. I say, "If I can show you how to take a business that's making $10,000 a month in revenue to potentially doing $128,000 per month in revenue, when I can show you the math, will you be happy with me? Would you want me to keep working with you? Or would you rather I go work with your competitor?" You can argue with a lot of things and win, but math isn't one of them—show them the math. If they don't buy, they are dumb as a box of rocks, and they're not going to pay you anyway.

Nothing I shared with you is theory. Everything I shared with you is exactly what I do and what my clients have done. I just pulled back the curtain and showed you what the magician knows, so it doesn't have to be magic to you anymore.

Money is energy

Since we've talked a lot about money, let's get one thing out of the way. Money is spiritual.

ZERO TO FREEDOM SECRETS

What do I mean by that? Money is not material in its essence. Money, instead, is spiritual in nature. People say, "I don't want to be rich. I'm not materialistic." Well, which is it? You don't want to be rich, or you're not that materialistic? Remember, money is not material in its essence any more than human beings are material in their essence. Physical money is simply a representation of a particular value. It looks material, but its essence is spiritual. It can't go anywhere. It flows through space and time.

Let me explain further. If I have a penny and a $100 bill, which one is worth more? The penny or the $100 bill? Some say the penny is worth more because the material penny made out of metal is worth more than the paper a $100 bill is printed on.

How is it possible? Because the value of money is not based on the material it's made of. So what is the value of money? The value of money is based on the message it carries. In other words, language, and language is spiritual. You see, only spiritual beings have language.

We can tell how much a unit of money is worth based on what's printed on it. If it says $0.01, the money is worth one cent of a dollar. If the unit of money says $100, then it's worth 10,000 times the value of a penny.

Another proof that makes me think money is spiritual is that its value is not based on anything materialistic. We can also take it even further by saying that only spiritual things can be in more than one place at a time. Think about it. You can have money in your bank account, a checkbook in your desk drawer, and a debit card for that account, and they all represent the same money. How can that money be in two places at once?

Because money is critical. If you desire to increase the amount of money you earn, you must learn to operate on a higher spiritual level.

Now that you understand that money is energy and you need to operate on a higher spiritual level, we're going to talk about how to use *Spiritual Selling* to grow your business.

STEP 6
Spiritual Selling

"Stop selling, start serving."
-Zig Ziglar

Transformation

Yeah, I know you might be thinking, *What does spiritual selling have to do with any of this?*

Let me tell you a story. When I was in Costa Rica, I had the best vibes ever. Everyone was so chill. It's like people there understand the real meaning of life. In fact, they actually call it "Pura Vida," which technically means pure life.

In reality, it's very difficult to explain. It's like a concept of just being, just living, just making the most of it. It's a phrase that you hear all the time there. When they see you, they say, "Pura Vida." To say goodbye, they say, "Pura Vida." If you ask them how they are, they say, "Pura Vida." It's all about living this pure life and being in the present. It's all about the connection with your real self and understanding what your real self wants: Stay in the moment. You don't need any external validation; you have your internal knowing. You don't need to seek security or comfort or ease. You're happy to embrace the uncertainty, the pain, and the challenges because those are part of life. So you take them in a good way. The foundation is not fear or confusion or perfectionism or procrastination; the foundation is courage or confidence or action or being.

I'd probably say "being" a lot. Because this goes back to the concept "Be-Do-Have." And whatever you're selling is always a transformation. Whatever transformation you want to help people to have, it needs to start with being. They need to become that person.

That is why I call it spiritual selling.

We're talking about selling because if you want to have your financial freedom, your location freedom, and your time freedom, you need to change a lot of lives.

And you need to do this by touching your spiritual being. And to do this, you need to get good at selling. Selling is not talking people into buying things they don't want, need, or can't afford.

Selling is uncovering the value of what you have to offer so well that people are happy to exchange the money they have in their pocket for the value you've revealed.

What does it mean to uncover value? The problem is when we think about uncovering value to people, we think about uncovering what's valuable to us or our "thing." But that's not the same thing as uncovering value to people. Why? Because they don't care about your "thing." And don't worry, it's not just you. They don't care about my "thing" either. They don't like you that much. And again, sorry for that, but that's the truth. They don't like me that much. I'm just keeping it real. They like themselves—period.

Nobody will listen to you talk to them about your stuff because they don't care. Before you can offer something of value to someone, you must uncover what's valuable to that person. In order to uncover the value of what's valuable to that someone, you have to ask questions and wait for answers, or you at least have to pay attention to what people are complaining about. People only pay you for solving their problems. They're not going to pay you for solving the problems you want to solve.

You might be thinking, *Yeah, but I always wanted to do this.*

That's nice. Make it a hobby. It doesn't deserve to be your business. You want to solve problems that people know they have.

As we've discussed in the five Ps earlier, the bigger the problem is to the person, the larger the amount of money they will pay you for solving it. And the bigger the transformation will be. Because remember, you're helping people transform. In fact, something very important is that you're not selling a process. It's not the *process* you're selling. What you're selling is the *payoff*. The payoff is the answer they're looking for, and the process is the way to get the payoff or the transformation. You don't sell them the process. You sell them the payoff and then deliver the process. If I have time to sell you by showing you my process, the conclusion you're going to come to on a conscious or subconscious level is, *It's too hard*, so you're not going to buy it. I never sell the process. People only get to learn my process after buying, and that payoff will be the transformation.

Remember at the beginning where we said that your process is how to help them to go from point A to point B? That is the transformation, the transformation of their being. Following your process will help them become the person they need to be, to do the things they need to do to have the transformation they want to have, and arrive at point B. You're selling the spiritual transformation.

Offers and Value

Now that we understand why people buy, let's talk about offers and their value. I sell mostly what are known as high ticket, which I like to think of as high-value products and services. This is my playground, and this is the arena where I'm one of the best, especially if you combine high ticket with freedom. There might be other growth coaches selling, teaching how to sell high ticket, but very few of them have the freedom that I have and that I teach my students to achieve. I also sell some lower price products. I sell for one purpose, which is to impact more people to the point that they can afford to invest in the premium offers to impact them even more.

I've got three offers: One is a low ticket offer, and two are premium offers. I also recommend you have some premium offers if you don't have them yet. One of my offers is $97 per month; that's the little one. One of them is $7,500, and my big premium offer is $36,000 to join the "Growers Club."

It might seem crazy to you that I got an offer where a client paid me $36.000 at once.

It seemed crazy to me too to be honest because in one day I made what I used to make in a year working in a marketing agency in London.

Here is what I know, the main reason you've never sold a product for $36,000 is that you don't have one to sell. Is that the only reason? Maybe not the only reason, but definitely the main reason.

Do you know why you don't have one to sell? Because you never thought about the problem of a premium buyer more than they have to the point where you understand it at the highest level and can persuasively explain to them why your solution is their best chance to get the payoff they desire.

Read that again.

You've never crafted a message showing your ideal client that your solution is worth so much more than the money they are about to pay you. They will pay you and thank you in tears for giving them the opportunity to buy.

When I'm creating an offer, the first question I ask myself is how much money do I want to make when I sell it, not how much money do I think I can make. How much money do I want to make for this thing? That's the first question I ask myself. Let's say that the answer is $36,000.

My second question is how can I produce a $360,000 result for someone's investment and make it so apparent that it is the best chance to get the outcome they've been seeking that they are happy to pay me regardless of the price? And by the way, that will not come to me in five minutes. If it takes me five days or five weeks to figure out how to produce a $306,000 result, isn't it worth it?

There are very few things you will do in your life that are more valuable. Your problem is that you want to run to the marketplace with an underdeveloped offer for an undervalued price, and then you get mad at the goal because you're struggling.

Don't do that anymore. Take the time on the front end to make your offer valuable when you present it in the marketplace. I like premium value markets because I set the price. If for no other reason, that's enough, I set the price. And because you're starting with organic Secret Attraction Marketing, you have the chance to talk more with your clients, which generally doesn't happen when you start to pay to advertise.

If I'm going to have a business and I'm the one doing the work in the business, doesn't it make sense that I should be the one setting the price? I mean, am I missing something? I set the price because I'm the one who has to do the work. I'm the one who's going to produce the result. So maybe, just maybe, I should set the price. That's one reason I like premium value markets.

Another reason I like premium value markets is that all of the conversations happen before the customers buy, and it happens with me and only me. Because of that, I get to reveal the value before I reveal the price. They know how valuable it is long before they know what the price is. When I do visual seminars or master classes, and I make my $36,000 offer, they have to accept the offer before they know what the price is, before they know what the pieces are, and before they know what the process is. How is that possible? It's possible because I take a day and a half of my life (sometimes two or three) to reveal to them the payoff. They don't know what the price is. They don't know what the pieces are. The one thing they know is the payoff. They already know it's not cheap because I already told them that. They know it's going to be less than a house, but definitely more than $199, because I told them, and they said yes.

In fact, I have the people who say yes stay in the Zoom room and have everyone else clap for them. And they still don't know what they said yes to or how much it costs. They only know the payoff, but they're excited to say yes to the payoff. Do you know what I have everyone else in the Zoom Room to do if they do *not* say yes? Leave the room. Go to lunch or dinner. The people who do not take the offer don't even get to find out what the offer is. I'm telling you, that is how the conversation happens even before they know the price. That is how you sell the premium value markets, but you have to be willing to do it in that order. And when you do that, you create premium value.

I'll create my own premium value market. What else do I do to create the premium value? I give results in advance. I call this "results in advance" Marketing. To do "results in advance" marketing, you need to create what is called a master class or challenges or virtual seminar, or webinar. They're all the same thing.

In this book, I'm not going to be able to go into the details, but if you're thinking about creating your own master class, feel free to go to www.zerotofreedomsecrets.com/freegifts And I will give you the exact step-by-step we use to make $10,000 a day using master classes and master class three or two-day challenges or seminars. As I said, they're all different. One, done correctly, is a way to give people results in advance. If you are following me on Facebook or Instagram, you'll see that I do this kind of master class every month where people get results in advance, and I have them do the first step.

Remember that I told you to think about point A, then think about point B and the steps they need to take to achieve point B? Perfect. Give them the first step. If the first step is too complicated or insufficient, give them the second step.

If the first two steps are not valuable enough, give them the first three steps.

The point is to give them enough steps to get started.

Give them a way to get the first results so they can start thinking, "Wow, if Bruno helped me to get this result in advance without even paying, and just using this free masterclass or free challenge, imagine the benefit and the growth and the progress I will have when I invest in the program." That is the thinking that you want them to have, and why I do community service work.

That does not mean I go around picking up trash in the neighborhood. It means that I have a Facebook Group where I give a lot of value. I create content on Instagram and my other social media to give massive value. I put out free content. And if I do say so myself, my free content is better than a lot of other people's content—I'm not lying.

When some people put out free content, they want to put out free junk. And then people never get a chance to experience the good stuff that they have for sale. I give **a** lot of transformational strategies for free, and they say, "If he taught me this much for free, how much will he teach me if I pay him?" Bottom line, figure out what your offer is and make that offer. Everything is about that offer.

Making a lot of money and acquiring financial freedom is not hard.

It's actually quite simple. My business generates seven figures a year, and I work part-time. So I know making a lot of money is not the hard part.

The hard part is becoming the person who can do the thing that makes you a lot of money and gives you a lot of freedom.

That's why the beginning of this book was all about mindset, performance routines and productivity

For now, I want you to remember that the first thing you should do when you get started in a business is to begin at the end and work your way backward. Start with the end in mind. What does that mean? Figure out a high-value result you can create for a business owner and start with a high ticket offer. That's the best business advice I can give you.

Start with a premium high ticket offer.

You might be thinking, *I'm going to work my way up to a high ticket offer. I'm going to sell a $97 thing. Then a $297 thing and a $697 thing*, etc. My advice is to figure out a high value result you can produce for somebody and go charge them the money—don't be scared.

Now, you might be thinking: "*Is this enough? H*ow can I make an offer I'm not too confident about?"

I'm going to let you into a little secret. If you don't make the offer, then it's already a no. Since I already got a no, I can either keep the no or I can give myself a chance to get a yes.

Are you picking up what I'm putting down? Just remember, an offer you don't make is an offer they can't take. Alright?

Freedom

Look for the opportunity to leap, and leap faster than your fear can grab you. Leap before you talk yourself out of it, before you convince yourself to set up a temporary camp that turns into a permanent delay on your journey into your own heart." -Vironika Tugaleva

Now you know all the steps *from zero to freedom.*

They say, "Look before you leap." So look. But do not look for too long. Do not look into the void of uncertainty trying to predict each and every possible outcome, to evaluate every possible mistake, to prevent each possible failure.

Your ego will try to hold you back.

Your parents will try to hold you back.

Some of your friends will try to hold you back.

I need to warn you that every time you're about to level up, you're getting ready to go to another level. And that is overwhelming. It's kind of like driving a car with an automatic transmission. When you're going at a certain speed in a certain gear, the engine starts revving up, and what happens? You don't say, "Oh my goodness, my engine is about to blow."

No, it just lets you know that the engine is about to change gears. It's about to go into a higher gear.

When you start to feel overwhelmed, you start thinking, *Oh my goodness, this is too much. I don't know if I can make it. I just feel overwhelmed right now.* But what you've got to understand is that when you start feeling those feelings, they are nothing more than a sign that you are getting ready to shift into a higher year. When you start feeling overwhelmed, understand that "overwhelm" is not a sign that you should quit. "Overwhelm" is a sign that you're about to level up. You're getting ready to go to another level.

While resistance sometimes manifests as overwhelming, it can also manifest as judgment. Judgment can, in fact, manifest through your thinking that something is too difficult for you. Sometimes judgment manifests as thinking something is too easy. If you find yourself thinking, *I don't know why I have to do this or that. I'm smarter than that.* That's resistance masked as judgment.

Do you realize there are things in your life right now that you think are too hard for you to do? And the truth is, the only reason you think they're too hard is that you've never properly learned how to do that.

You realize there is nothing really that hard to do. What's hard is thinking about needing to do something that you don't know how to do and feeling like you have to do it before you learn how to do it.

I promise you there is nothing that's too hard for you to learn if you learn it step-by-step. That is why I just gave you those steps. When I said that every time you feel overwhelmed is a sign that you're about to level up is part of the same steps that you need to do to level up. Which is to start finding your "why." Understand what's your freedom number and have a clear vision of what is your financial freedom, your location freedom, and time freedom. Then you want to become that person that gets to do the things that you need to do in order to have the things that you want to have.

As soon as you become that person, you'll need to do a specific number of things. You need to be productive in what you're doing. Here's where you incorporate the five Ps to make sure that you understand clearly your purpose, your power, your potential, your passion, and the problems that you're solving.

Then when that is clear, you will again be ready to level up. And then you're going to create your magnetic offer that is so magnetic it attracts the right people for you, and then you start to turn those problems into solutions by creating trainings that transform. And then, after creating your magnetic offer, you will be ready to level up.

You're going to start growing your business with Secret Attraction Marketing. And after growing your business with Secret Attraction Marketing, you will need to improve at spiritual selling. And when you get better at spiritual selling, I can guarantee you, I literally guarantee this to my students, you're going to achieve your definition of financial freedom, location freedom, and time freedom.

What you do have is the right way to grow. You first become that person, then you get to do the things to have the things that you want. The dream life, the dream house, the dream sex, the dream partner, the time freedom, the financial freedom, and the location freedom all start with you becoming that person. Remember to start with the end in mind. Start with a very high value magnetic offer and work your way back. Make sure that you choose the way you deliver based on the freedom that you want to get.

If you're happy to help people in a group session, then you're going to be able to maximize your time freedom by doing only one or two hours of group sessions a week. If you're just starting out, you may need to go through the done-*for*-you where you are doing the work first for them, and only then will you be able to move to the done-*with*-you or do-it-*yourself* model by gradually increasing your freedom.

Consulting freedom is one of the best models because it's the one that really helps you decide the price, the time you're going to work, the location where you're going to work from, and the impact that you're going to have on the world, in your family and yourself.

You must learn only to expect the outcomes that you desire.

You might be thinking, *I like the idea of that, but how do I do that?*

By having a burning desire, a visualization of you achieving it already.

Everything is energy. Money is spiritual, and energy is neither created nor destroyed—it just changes form. That's a physics principle. May I give you another physics principle? No high-energy result will ever flow to a low-energy source. By the way, wealth is a high-energy result, which means that unless you bring all the energy you've got to everything you do, you have no hope of creating wealth. That's what you've got to do: become a high-energy source.

Raise your right hand and say this out loud. "I will... for the rest of my life... be a high energy source."

Now say this out loud. "Anything I tell myself about a future outcome, I made it up." Did you catch that? *Anything you tell yourself about the future outcome, you made it up.*

When we get into our cars to go home, we think, *Well, I'm going home.* We really mean that we intend to go home, but the reality is that do we know for sure we're going to make it home? No, but we believe we will make it home because if we didn't, we wouldn't leave. We'd stay there. Hang in there with me.

So I borrow energy. I don't even borrow it. I just grab some energy from the future. And when I grab some energy from the future, and I use that energy from the future to take action in the present, that makes that future thing manifest.

So instead of asking, *what if it doesn't work?* I ask myself, *How awesome is this going to be when it works? How amazing is my life going to be when this works? How awesome will it be when my business starts making $10,000 a month or $128,000? (Or whatever is your freedom number)*

And I tell myself, *When I build this business, it will be great. I'm going to have the freedom that I always wanted.*

Now it's time to make the decision. When you make a decision, you cut yourself off from every other possibility. If you have not yet become the person who can do the thing, you first need to decide to do it, which is not the same as choosing to do it. The word "choose" means to pick one. The word "decide" is a compound D meaning "off" or "from," and "cide," meaning "to cut out."

Now *you* decide. You cut yourself off from all other options. You literally go all in. Go all in.

When you make the decision to go all in to achieve your definition of freedom, you can't fail because it is only a matter of time.

Trying is what guarantees you're going to have success. A lot of people make a choice. They are making a decision. Decisions create confidence. What does that mean? The root of the word confidence is the word "confide." The word confide means to trust. The reason people don't have confidence is that they cannot confide in themselves. They don't trust themselves. Why don't people trust themselves? Because they've broken their words so many times, they can't believe a word they say.

Every time you let yourself off the hook, you are breaking a covenant with yourself. Understand that a covenant is an agreement between two or more individuals based upon mortal law and trust. When you make a covenant with someone, you swear on your existence to keep that promise. And you're saying, *I would rather die in honor and keep my worth than live in dishonor and break my promise.*

When you learn to make decisions that, in reality, are a covenant with yourself, you will begin to trust yourself, and you will have the confidence to go out and become the person who can do the "thing."

People ask, "What should I do?"

If I tell you what to do? You're not going to do it until you become the person who can do it. We don't send our two-year-old granddaughter to her room to clean it. She has not yet become the person who can do it. Does that make sense?

Did you know that the biggest challenge you have in doing whatever it is that you want to do with your business, whether it's growing it to $100,000, $1 million, $10 million, or whatever your goal is, the biggest problem you have is that you have not yet become the person who can do it. And unfortunately, you've been programmed by a system designed to program you to fail. By fail, I mean quit working towards your goal.

You'll do something for 15 minutes or 15 days or 15 weeks, or 15 months, and when it doesn't produce the results you thought it should produce, you say it didn't work.

I have good news for you. There is no such thing as work that doesn't work. All work works, but work is a two-sided coin. If things don't work *for* you, they're working *on* you first.

It might be working *for* you, but it's not working *on* you.

It might *not* be working *for* you, but it's working *on* you.

Sometimes when things work *for* you a lot, they don't work *on* you nearly as much. I know you want it to work *for* you, but you're better off when it works *on* you. Because when you become the person who can do the "thing" repeatedly, then it doesn't matter what happens. It doesn't matter if Facebook takes away your Facebook page. It doesn't matter if Instagram blocks you or your post. It doesn't matter if something interrupts your business or the marketplace changes. It doesn't matter because you become the person who can do the "thing."

The most important work I ever do is the work I do on myself. Why? Because that's how God set it up from the beginning. In the beginning, God created this platform for us to operate as human beings. It governs our experience of life. You say, "I don't believe in God." That's all right. It's going to be alright. He's feeling good. It's going to be okay. That is why all this is important because making more of the wrong moves doesn't make you richer. It just makes you more tired.

A lot of people have been programmed to believe that working hard is the solution. But working hard is only the solution if you're working hard on the thing that will produce the biggest outcome.

Many people also make the mistake of thinking that work is something God gave to man as a punishment for sin. That's not true. Work is something God gave man because man was created in the image of God.

Before God created man, he created the heavens and the earth. When I first read that in Scripture, I wondered, *Why would He create the heavens and earth?* The only answer I've been able to find is that he is creative. Therefore, His nature is to create. That means the first thing the Bible tells us about God is that God is creative. The first thing God tells a man about men is that he created us in His image, which means he created us to create stuff, and He made us to make stuff.

God put work in the world for man to do before he put man in the world to do the work. *God put work in the world for man to do before he put man in the world to do the work.* That means business is a good idea. Business is a good idea when you believe that you are created in the image of someone whose nature is to create, and you discover your purpose at the intersection of your passion, and your superpower will empower you to build and scale the consulting freedom business of your dreams.

Conclusion and Next Steps

First and foremost, allow me to congratulate you on finishing this book. These days, it is a very rare person who starts to read a book on one's own volition, especially on how to scale a business and achieve your definition of freedom.

As the saying goes, "It's the start that stops most people." Congratulations for not letting the start stop you.

So few people will even begin a book to make their lives better. A much smaller number will read the book to its end. Ultimately, I hope and expect that you will take it a step further and become the person who implements what you've read to the point of mastery.

As an entrepreneur or aspiring entrepreneur, you will likely find yourself stuck in one or two categories. If you're in category one, you're stuck generating less than $5,000 per month. If this is where you find yourself, your cost of action will be a simple one. You must learn and master the four pillars that can grow a business. You must master lead generation, lead conversion, customer ascension, and customer retention. You can learn to master these four moves through trial and error or allow me and my team to assist you in this journey and potentially shave years off the learning curve.

If you would like us to assist you in scaling your business to $12,000 per month and beyond, join our membership. At the time of this writing, we run our monthly membership at just $97. You can register at the website below, and you'll be able to meet me live for one hour per week, three weeks a month, and get your individual questions answered via a Zoom meeting.

Go to www.zerotofreedomsecrets.com to take the next step in changing your life.

If you're in category two, you're an entrepreneur stuck between $12,000 and $100,000 per month in revenue. If that's where you find yourself right now, we can help. We have a mastermind of extremely high level entrepreneurs, many of whom were stuck between $5,000 and $100,000 per month in revenue. We've helped many get to $20,000 to $100,000 per month. We've even had some clients scale their business to $1 million a year.

While it's obvious that neither I nor anyone else can guarantee these results, or any results for that matter, I think we can agree that you can increase your chance of these kinds of results if you are in an environment where they are passionately pursued and achieved.

If you want guidance and direction on the way to your business goals, we will be honored to assist you on this journey. I have created a coaching mastermind in which I teach my clients the model to achieve your Declaration of Freedom. When my students apply these principles to their businesses, they experience exponential growth, exponential freedom, and exponential impact, both personally and professionally. If you'd like to know more about this program and see if you qualify, go to our website, **www.sam-mentoring.com.**

THANK YOU FOR READING MY BOOK!

DOWNLOAD YOUR FREE GIFTS

Just to say thanks for buying and reading my book, I would like to give you a few free bonus gifts, no strings attached!

To Download Now, Visit:
www.ZerotoFreedomSecrets.com/Freegifts

I appreciate your interest in my book, and I value your feedback as it helps me improve future versions of this book. I would appreciate it if you could leave your invaluable review on Amazon.com with your feedback. Thank you!

www.ingramcontent.com/pod-product-compliance
Lightning Source LLC
Chambersburg PA
CBHW072204090426
42740CB00012B/2383